CRAG WORKING GROUP ON MENTAL ILLNESS

Primary Prevention of Mental Health Problems

December 1995

FOREWORD

We hope this Position Statement will prove useful to initiate discussion on primary prevention between those who provide, purchase and receive mental health care.

The Statement reflects the views of health professionals, managers and users of mental health services throughout Scotland, and has been endorsed by the CRAG Working Group on Mental Illness and by CRAG.

Karen N. Foster

Dr Karen Foster
Chairperson
Good Practice Group on Primary Prevention

Angus Mackay

Dr Angus VP Mackay
Chairman
CRAG Working Group on Mental Illness

Robert Kendell

RE Kendell
Chairman CRAG

Contents

1. REMIT

The group was established in December 1994 with the following remit:-

1. To produce guidelines to meet the needs of all organisations and individuals responsible for purchasing health care services.

2. To identify an appropriate route for disseminating the information in the document to purchasers in Scotland and other appropriate agencies.

3. To facilitate the development of appropriate research.

4. To encourage the implementation of effective interventions.

5. To encourage the development of health alliances with other agencies who can influence social and economic issues affecting mental health.

Terminology

The terminology used in this document is discussed in Appendix A, and for reasons argued there the term 'mental health problem' will be used in preference to terms such as 'disorder' or 'illness' except where there are direct quotes from other authors.

2. BACKGROUND

2.1 Size of the problem

Mental health problems are a leading cause of distress, disability and death. Mental health problems have been shown to affect one in four of the United Kingdom population at any point in time[1] and make significant demands on the NHS, social services, employers and society in general, accounting for approximately 14 per cent of NHS costs and approximately 14 per cent of days lost at work.[2] A recent survey by the Office of Population Censuses and Surveys (OPCS) found that about one in seven adults aged 16 to 64 living in private households in Great Britain had a neurotic mental health problem in the week prior to interview.[3] Morbidity is commonly found in the carers of patients with mental health problems, who often develop problems themselves or have pre-existing mental health problems.[2]

The cut off point between what is considered normal distress or behaviour and a mental health problem is often blurred as different standards of normality may apply at different times in different social and ethnic groups and by geographical location. This means that mental health problems can be difficult to define and estimates of prevalence will therefore vary depending on the diagnostic criteria used.

2.2 Prevention

Primary prevention involves measures aimed at reducing the incidence (rate of occurrence of new cases) of a disease or disorder. Thus the primary prevention of mental health problems is defined as actions intended to reduce the incidence of mental health problems amongst people who are relatively free of distressing psychiatric symptoms or who are suffering from symptoms not extensive and severe enough to be defined as cases.[4] They may never before have experienced mental health problems or they may have largely recovered from previous problems. Primary preventive measures are therefore directed at people who are not experiencing symptoms but who are believed to be at risk of developing a mental health problem.

Secondary prevention aims to halt the progression of a disorder once it is established and includes the detection and treatment of first and recurrent episodes of mental health problems. This paper is concerned **only** with primary prevention.

Prevention may be achieved either by eliminating the cause and/or enhancing host resistance.

2.3 Epidemiological framework

Epidemiological studies have identified variables which are associated with the development of mental health problems but in many cases the causal relationship is far from clear. Further, there is a difference between those variables associated with mental health problems in an individual or groups of individuals and those associated with overall levels of mental health problems in a population.[5] For example, there has been a marked increase in the incidence of depressive disorders in young adults over the last thirty years.[6] While genetic factors play a role in an individual's risk of developing depression, they do not explain the large increase in depression at the population level and other causes must be sought. Most mental health problems have multi-factorial causes and prevention must take account of this. Before prevention can occur it must be possible to show that causal factors can be modified sufficiently to have an impact on the causal process.

It is often assumed that prevention will reduce future treatment costs. However, most people with mental health problems are never seen by a psychiatrist and many do not consult any health care professionals.[1] An effective prevention programme might therefore have little effect on the number of patients seen or might increase overall health service costs. It will, however, reduce the wider social costs resulting from mental health problems.

Studies of overall levels of mental health in populations have shown that there is a continuum between mental health and mental health problems. The average level of mental health varies between regions, genders, social classes and income groups. These differences are due to shifts of the entire distribution of mental health rather than changes in dispersion. It follows that the difference in the prevalence of mental health problems between populations reflects the differing

3

states of mental health in the parent populations. For example, the greater the depression score in a population, the greater the number of individuals at the upper end of the distribution curve who will require treatment for depressive syndrome.

2.4   Alternative approaches to prevention

Two approaches to prevention have been described, the high-risk strategy and the population-based strategy. The high-risk strategy attempts to identify individuals at particularly high risk for specific disorders, enabling highly specific preventive approaches for a relatively small population. The population-based strategy aims to control the determinants of incidence, to lower the mean level of risk factors and shift the whole distribution of exposure in a favourable direction. A preventive policy which focuses on high risk individuals may benefit those individuals greatly but will have little impact on the total burden of disease in the population. Alternatively, a successful population-based policy will lower the whole distribution of exposure levels, giving everyone in the population a slightly lower risk, but will not be as beneficial to the smaller number of individuals at high risk.[7] The complementary relationship between the two approaches is reflected in this report.

2.5   Potential for effective action

The following sections of the report will consider what is known about the causes of mental health problems and the potential for effective prevention. There are many areas where primary prevention of mental health problems would be valuable. This document will identify only those areas where published studies which describe the effectiveness of primary preventive interventions indicate that these areas are worthy of further investigation. For many conditions there is no published evaluation of primary preventive interventions and for many more the little published work that exists shows that interventions have been ineffective to date. If an area is not described in this document it does not mean that the Working Group did not consider it. It simply means that no work has been published to indicate that primary prevention in that area appears to be worthy of further investigation at this time.

An exception to this is mental health in the workplace which is being dealt with by a sub-group of the Scottish Needs Assessment Programme (SNAP).

The primary prevention of suicide will not be dealt with as a specific topic in this document, because the remit of the Working Group is to consider the primary prevention of mental health problems. In many cases individuals who attempt or complete suicide have been suffering from a mental health problem, but this is not always so. Reducing the incidence of mental health problems should lead to a reduction in the number of suicides which are related to such problems. However, the work of other groups should be consulted for a full discussion of the prevention of suicide.[8]

Environmental biological causes will not be dealt with either as there are other fora in which there is discussion of the prevention of nutritional deficiency, trauma, infection and atherosclerosis etcetera in a more comprehensive manner.

Finally, this document will not review the primary prevention of learning disabilities.

3. THE CAUSES OF MENTAL HEALTH PROBLEMS

The causes of mental health problems can be separated into two broad but overlapping categories, biological and psychosocial.

3.1 Biological causes

Biological causes include genetic causes and environmental biological causes such as nutrition, trauma, infections, toxicity and atherosclerosis. Genetic causes will be dealt with briefly in this paper.

There is strong evidence of a genetic contribution to schizophrenia, bipolar manic depressive disorder and autism, moderately strong evidence for more severe unipolar depressions and suggestive evidence for anxiety and personality disorders, alcoholism and certain childhood disorders.[9] However, the genetic contribution only partly explains these conditions. Environmental factors play an important role, notably for more severe unipolar depressive syndromes and alcoholism.

Single genes of major effect have been identified for some specific learning disability syndromes, Huntington's disease and certain forms of pre-senile Alzheimer's disease.[9]

Specialist genetic counselling services should therefore be available on a regional basis to provide information on genetic risk and enable individuals/couples to make informed decisions about psychiatric conditions with a genetic component.

3.2 Psychosocial causes

Psychosocial and biological causes interact in complex and, as yet, not fully understood ways. Psychosocial causes tend to be separated into early and recent effects, although in reality the effect of the psychosocial environment is a continuous one.

The clearest links between adverse childhood experiences and adult disorder are seen for affective and personality disorders. Such experiences largely consist of serious disruptions in the quality and consistency of parenting. It is the persistence of such circumstances rather than their initial occurrence which influences future development of disorders.[9]

Recent adverse life events have been shown to be associated with the timing of onset of a range of mental health problems, including post traumatic disorders, depressive disorder, schizophrenia and anxiety disorders.[9,10]

Prevention of psychosocial causes of mental health problems can be directed at a variety of levels; the individual, the family, the immediate social network and society at large. Preventive efforts can be aimed at those individuals whose vulnerability is increased by such situations or at reducing/eliminating psychosocial stress. These approaches are complementary.

Purchasers have a limited direct role to play in the reduction/elimination of social stress and influencing society at large. Interventions at this level are clearly political rather than clinical. In the field of mental health, unemployment, poverty and poor housing or homelessness have been shown to be associated with mental health problems.[4,10-12] In Scotland, the Third Monica Survey in Glasgow provides evidence of the extent to which depression and anxiety are socially patterned. Levels of both depression and anxiety were shown to increase with increasing deprivation scores.[13]

Purchasers should, however, work in partnership with agencies which are responsible for policies in these areas. This work should include highlighting the potentially adverse health effects of social policies, encouraging and supporting research aimed at quantifying the adverse effects, identifying alternative policies which would promote health and encouraging the implementation of such policies by all relevant agencies. NHS resources should be used in the main to address those factors which can be influenced by health services. Other agencies should be encouraged to develop their role in areas more appropriately dealt with outside the NHS, e.g. self-help groups and voluntary organisations. However, these agencies may require support and assistance from the NHS in order to do so.

4. ESTABLISHING THE EFFECTIVENESS OF PRIMARY PREVENTION STRATEGIES

It is becoming increasingly important for purchasers to demonstrate that the services they purchase are effective. Resources are limited and purchasing one type of service means those resources are not available to be used in other competing areas (opportunity costs).

The gold standard for measuring the effectiveness of any intervention is the randomised controlled trial (RCT) although some authorities challenge the appropriateness of using RCTs in the study of psychological interventions. While there are many examples of initiatives aimed at preventing mental health problems, rigorous evaluations of services are rare, as are economic evaluations. One reason for this is that the evaluation of preventive mental health services is fraught with methodological, practical and ethical difficulties.[4,14] The main methodological problems include:-

1. The use of small study populations.

2. Selection bias in choosing intervention and control groups.

3. The failure to allocate randomly to intervention and control groups.

4. The failure to identify which specific elements of an intervention are effective and failure to match appropriate interventions to individuals/groups.

5. The Hawthorne effect (ie. the effects of being under study on the persons being studied, usually positive or beneficial).

6. Poor uptake and high attrition rates (although this may be less of a concern if this is what happens in practice).

7. The failure to identify correct timing both for implementing the intervention and measuring the outcome.

8. The uncertain validity of measures used both for selecting a high risk population and measuring the outcome.

9. Short length of follow-up and measurement of intermediate risk factor status rather than disease-related outcomes.

Limiting the determination of effectiveness to those studies which meet the criteria for RCTs (quantitative studies) means that a large volume of relevant information is automatically excluded.

Qualitative studies may not meet the conventional criteria for effectiveness but can help to create a fuller understanding by exploring concepts of health and disease, examining other factors affecting health and health care and gaining insight into the processes through which preventive interventions may be effective.[15]

More direct discussion with and involvement of individuals who have experienced mental health problems may also assist researchers in exploring the causes of mental health problems, and assessing the potential for preventive interventions and the effect of any interventions.

5. EVIDENCE OF EFFECTIVE INTERVENTIONS

A rigorous literature review of all primary prevention strategies in the field of mental health would be highly resource intensive in terms of time and manpower. Such a review was quite outwith the capability of this group. Therefore the group chose as a starting point existing reviews of the literature which identified areas where evaluations of primary prevention strategies had been undertaken. The literature in these areas was then reviewed to verify the conclusions reached by the authors.

It appears that few primary preventive interventions in the field of mental health have been shown to be effective unequivocally. However, there are some areas where the results of evaluations are favourable and which may, with further research, be shown to be effective.

This paper will therefore indicate those interventions which appear to have promising results and which are worthy of further study and investment of resources. The paper will also highlight issues within mental health which are likely to assume increasing importance over the next few years and in which there has been little research or evaluation to date.

5.1 Under fives and their families

Risk factors for the development of mental health problems in children include biological factors, such as perinatal anomalies and chronic illness and psychosocial factors, such as family dysfunction, deprivation and social disadvantage.[4,9,16]

Not all childhood problems carry on into adulthood. Many have a good outcome in childhood, and many adult problems do not originate in childhood. However, it is known that early childhood experiences and the quality of parenting influence the later development of problems such as emotional disturbances, delinquent behaviour and psychiatric disorders, especially depression.[16-19] Poor parenting may also be associated with child abuse which itself can have psychiatric sequelae in adult life.

Research into primary preventive interventions in this area has focused on the early family environment and these interventions can be categorised into

❏ services to parents and children in the new born period and infancy, e.g. supportive care and information for the parents, feeding and stimulation for the children.[17,19,20]

❏ services to parents and children in the pre-school period, e.g. information on child development and parenting skills and social support for the parents, educational support for the children.[17,18,21]

There is evidence to suggest that such interventions which modify the early family environment and provide support may have a positive effect on cognitive development, behavioural problems, school achievement and anti-social behaviour/delinquency.[16-19,21] Such interventions appear most effective when applied to high risk groups (eg. low socio-economic class, single/young parent) and early prevention strategies (ie. pre-school) may be more effective than later ones. Programmes aimed at behavioural rather than affective or cognitive change may be more successful in changing the behaviour of children than the behaviour of parents. Boys in at-risk environments respond better to preventive interventions than girls.

Examples of the above interventions which have published evaluations include:-

❏ The Newpin Programme (United Kingdom) which aimed to alleviate maternal depression by providing a volunteer supportive and befriending scheme.[22,23]

❏ The Head Start Intervention Programme (USA) which provided information for parents and pre-school education to low income families with 3 to 4 year old children.[18]

❏ The Perry Pre-School Programme (USA), a variety of Head Start, which provided pre-school education for children and support to parents.[21]

❏ The Houston Parent-Child Development Centre (USA) which was designed to help low income Mexican/American families who were at risk for child behavioural problems.[24]

❑ The Carolina Abecedarian Project (USA) which screened patients in a pre-natal clinic to select those families with risk factors who were then provided with a child-centred systematic educational programme in a daycare setting.[25]

A Scottish example is Home-Start (UK) which trains and supports volunteers who offer friendship and practical help to young families under stress.

Generalisation from these studies cannot be assumed as they were high quality demonstration projects with low sample sizes and high staff to child ratios, which were under pressure to show research results. It is important that their effectiveness is assessed by replication of the projects in diverse populations with long-term follow-up assessments. Future research should also aim to identify the characteristics of populations who would benefit from such preventive strategies, which elements of the strategies have a meaningful and measurable effect and the most effective timing and duration of the strategy. Once the effectiveness of these programmes has been determined, the question of efficiency, i.e. costs and benefits, should be addressed by economic evaluations.

Some studies have specifically attempted to prevent child abuse by detecting high-risk families and providing home visitation, largely by nursing staff.[20,26-29] The effectiveness of these initiatives has yet to be established but many are not resource intensive and, if shown to be clinically effective, may also prove to be cost effective. However, care must be taken in the implementation of such programmes so as not to stigmatise the participants as being at high risk of child abuse. Fear of stigmatisation might reduce uptake, thereby reducing the effectiveness of the programme as well as causing distress to anxious parents.

5.2 School-based programmes and adolescence

A number of school-based primary prevention programmes have been undertaken.[4,16,18,30-32] These include competency-building programmes, which aim to teach important behaviours or skills to enhance children's functioning and prevent future problems, and programmes to reduce childhood aggression. There is insufficient evidence to establish the effectiveness of these programmes and further research is required.

Providing support for adolescents at vulnerable stages in their lives e.g. the transition to secondary school, may produce beneficial outcomes.[33,34] This area also requires further research.

Children looked after and accommodated in institutional care are at high risk of homelessness, pre-marital pregnancy, social difficulties and depression. Interventions have been aimed at supporting children during the transition to independence (First Key, Bradford After-Care Team) and supporting teenage girls during and after pregnancy (St Michael's Hostel).[4,35] All these initiatives have published favourable results, in terms of satisfaction with the project, but have not been properly evaluated to establish their effectiveness. Scottish examples of these initiatives include the Barnardos 16 plus project (Edinburgh) and the Walpole Housing Association (Edinburgh and Glasgow).

School-based suicide prevention programmes have been introduced, largely in the United States, to heighten awareness of the issue, enhance coping skills and provide crisis intervention services.[36-43] Their effectiveness has not been established. Some programmes showed positive results in terms of improving knowledge, attitudes and coping behaviours, with girls responding more favourably to the programmes than boys. However, the efficacy of these programmes in reducing the numbers of attempted/completed suicides in the long term remains unproven. There is also some indication that such programmes may "normalise" suicide behaviour and may, in some circumstances, actually increase the likelihood of attempted suicide.

5.3   Life events

Early intervention after life events to provide support and to facilitate coping mechanisms may be of great value in the prevention of affective disorders. However, further research is necessary before wide implementation of the following programmes could be recommended.

a.   **Post-natal Depression**. This subject will be dealt with in greater detail by the CRAG/SCOTMEG Working Group on Maternity Services. There is insufficient evidence to determine whether primary prevention of post-natal depression is possible although attempts have been made with the establishment of pregnancy support groups by health visitors and midwives.[44]

Children of women with post-natal depression are more likely to have behavioural problems and cognitive difficulties and to be at risk of physical abuse and accidental injuries.[45,46] Studies have shown that post-partum depressed women can be detected using the Edinburgh Post-natal Depression Scale (EPDS).[47] However, the use of a questionnaire should not replace listening to individual patients' problems. Health visitors have been successfully trained in the detection and management of post-natal depression.[48-50] Whilst this is a secondary prevention initiative for the women concerned, it may be a primary prevention of behavioural, cognitive and physical sequelae in children. However, there are no long-term studies to show that this is the case.

If successful, health visitor/midwife interventions are likely to be cost-effective initiatives in the primary and secondary prevention of post-natal depression.

b. **Bereavement**. There is evidence that interventions are effective in reducing the risk of the mental health problems which result from bereavement, particularly depressive disorders, panic and anxiety disorders.[51-56] These interventions are most effective when applied to a population at high risk of developing such adverse outcomes. There is no evidence of effectiveness in the general population. Risk factors associated with poor outcome after bereavement include; predisposing factors in the bereaved (eg. young age, low self-esteem, multiple prior losses); relationship to the deceased (eg. spouse, parent, ambivalence to/dependence on the deceased); mode of death (eg. unexpected, untimely, suicide, murder); social support absent or unhelpful.[57] The literature shows variations in the type of intervention (hospice volunteer counsellors, psychiatrist, other volunteer councillors and self-help groups) and the magnitude of differences observed. The type of professional involved will determine the cost and therefore the cost-effectiveness of the service. There is insufficient evidence to establish the most effective type of counsellor, setting for counselling or intensity/duration of the intervention. Populations studied have been mostly widows and widowers. Less is known about the applicability and effectiveness in other sub-populations such as sibling death, the death of a child and bereavement in various ethnic and cultural groups.[58]

c. **Cancer**. Studies have looked at the benefits of intervention with cancer patients to prevent mental health problems. Interventions include counselling by specialist nurses and cognitive behaviour treatment programmes.[59,60] The effectiveness of these interventions has not yet been established. More work is needed to determine the exact nature of the intervention and thus the training required. As cancer affects one in three of the population and is the cause of death of one in four, any interventions which alleviate distress and prevent morbidity would be of great value. This is clearly an area which would benefit from carefully evaluated projects.

d. **Post Traumatic Disorder.** Post Traumatic Disorder has been recognised as a sequela of severe psychological trauma in both children and adults.[61] Methodologically sound intervention studies are rare because of the unpredictable nature of trauma and disaster. Intervention before the event is necessarily restricted to groups/individuals at high risk: for example police, fire and army personnel.[62-66] After the event, primary prevention strategies may avoid the onset of the disorder in susceptible individuals. It has been suggested that the following strategies may be beneficial for individuals at high risk: preparation for stressful events, debriefing, fostering interpersonal relationships, good organisation and sensitive staff management practices.[62,63] However, there is a dearth of systematic evaluations and outcome studies.[67] Some studies show that subjects have found debriefing to be helpful yet there is little evidence of a positive effect on outcome. There are also some concerns that debriefing may have adverse effects by focusing on the trauma to the exclusion of other more relevant stressors, causing secondary traumatisation and medicalising normal responses to stress. Further work is also required to determine the best interventions for specific groups and incidents.

e. **Divorce**. Increasingly marital disruption is being recognised as a major stressful life event. Both the adults and children involved are at high risk of mental health problems. However, many of the adverse sequelae of divorce stem from the family conflict preceding the break-up of the marriage, rather than from the divorce as such. Studies describe interventions with both the newly separated and children of divorce. Interventions providing emotional support and facilitating competence building with the newly separated may lead to better adjustment, quality of life and fewer separation related problems in this group.[68,69] Programmes which provide support and facilitate skill building in children of divorce may improve adjustment and adaptive social skills while reducing problem behaviour.[70,71] As divorce now occurs in approximately one in three marriages, interventions which minimise the adverse effects would be of great value. Family Mediation Scotland is an example of an organisation which provides such interventions.

f.   **Unemployment.** Several studies have shown that unemployed people experience higher levels of depression, anxiety and general distress, together with lower self-esteem and confidence.[16,72-74] Continuing unemployment appears to be associated with further reductions in well-being. Unemployment has also been associated with a higher risk of suicide and parasuicide.[75-79] The effect of unemployment may be modified by social support and the maintenance of self-esteem.[72,80] The Preventive Job Search Intervention provided training for people unemployed less than six months with the aim of preventing the negative mental health effects of unemployment and promoting high quality re-employment.[15,81,82] The intervention reduced the likelihood that people at high risk experienced a severe episode of depression (and reduced the number of severe episodes by over one third) over a two year follow-up. High-risk status was predicted by pretest levels of depression, economic hardship and low social assertiveness.

5.4   Substance misuse

These will be dealt with briefly in this paper as the prevention of substance misuse is being dealt with more comprehensively in other fora.

Substance misuse is associated with a range of physical and psychiatric morbidity and in some cases death. It also results in social conflict in relation to family life, unemployment, accidents and criminal behaviour.

Prevention of such problems is not the remit of the NHS alone, but must be addressed by society as a whole. Primary prevention of substance misuse comprises two complementary measures, reduction of supply and reduction of demand.[83]

The reduction of supply involves strategies on statutory control and law enforcement, for example issues such as crop control, interception and interdiction, taxation and licensing laws. On the whole, any measures that make substances more readily available lead to an increase in the misuse of such substances. The role of the NHS in the reduction of supply involves initiatives to improve the appropriateness of prescribing of drugs which may be misused, such as barbiturates, amphetamines and benzodiazepines. Beneficial effects on suicide rates particularly impulse suicide may be achieved by actions to increase the safety of commonly used drugs, eg. decreasing the number of pills in a packet, packaging drugs in blister packs, reducing, by more appropriate prescribing, the ready availability of large quantities of toxic agents and even by the inclusion of an antidote in the drug formulation (such as methionine - with paracetamol).[8] The NHS must also work in alliance with other agencies to highlight the health implications of their policies and influence policy formation which will achieve health gain.

The reduction of demand involves educational initiatives, advertising controls and community responses which aim to minimise the likelihood of substance misuse occurring. All three measures require to be more fully evaluated to identify the most effective interventions.[83] The NHS should ensure that effective educational initiatives are used by all appropriate employees including Health Promotion staff, members of the primary care team and secondary care staff. Again, the NHS should work closely with other agencies to try to influence policies which lead to a reduction in demand.

6. CONCLUSIONS

Mental health problems cause a substantial amount of distress, morbidity and mortality. Primary preventive interventions aim to reduce the incidence of mental health problems either by targeting high risk individuals or by implementing population-wide strategies. The difficulty of first defining mental health problems and secondly identifying causal mechanisms makes it problematic to design appropriate preventive interventions.

The study of preventive mental health interventions is by its very nature fraught with methodological difficulties and rigorous evaluations are rare. However, there is some evidence that primary prevention may be effective in the following areas:-

1.   Under fives and their families

2.   Adolescence

3.   Life Events including Post-Natal Depression, Bereavement, Cancer, Severe and unusual Trauma, Divorce and Unemployment

4.   Substance Misuse

In none of these areas is there convincing evidence of effectiveness. All will require further research in larger diverse populations and in a service setting before true evidence of their effectiveness will be obtained.

It must be recognised that the direct role of the NHS in preventing mental health problems is limited. Mental health is affected by social polices and events which are largely outwith the control of the NHS. However, the NHS must develop health alliances to ensure that the health implications of decisions by other agencies are identified and addressed. Health alliances must be developed at both national and local levels to achieve the optimum outcomes.

7. RECOMMENDATIONS

7.1 Research

Further research should focus on areas, such as those above, where there is already some indication that interventions may be effective. Whilst the methodological difficulties in this field are recognised, attempts should be made to minimise these in any future research. In particular funding bodies should give priority to research proposals which meet the criteria for high quality quantitative research, i.e.

1. Large numbers and appropriate sample size calculations.

2. Random allocation to intervention and control groups.

3. Careful selection of participants to minimise bias, particularly the avoidance of self-selection.

4. Precise description of the nature of the intervention.

5. Use of valid tools to select high risk individuals and measure outcome.

6. Precise statement of intermediate and ultimate goals.

7. Long-term follow-up and measurement of disease-related outcomes.

8. Demonstration, within the intervention group, of a systematic relationship between the degree to which the intervention reduces the risk factor and the degree of benefit in terms of target disorder.

9. Inclusion of an economic evaluation.

More research is required into the determinants of effectiveness particularly the characteristics of both the programme and the target group which are predictive of effectiveness. The value of qualitative research in addressing these issues should be recognised. For example, in-depth interviews or participant observation can be used to explore people's experiences of an intervention. When qualitative research is used to explore such experience, it should be recognised that these experiences are an integral part of a social context from which they cannot be divorced and which must be understood from the respondent's perspective. The following are criteria for high quality exploratory research of this type:

1. Research questions should be framed as openly as possible so the researcher's own views intrude as little as possible.

2. Data should be explored in depth with respondents to help understand them from their perspective.

3. Inconsistencies in data should be explored to see how these make sense to the respondent, rather than treating them as 'true' or 'false'.

4. Data should not be divorced from their social context, for example by turning them into survey questions or quantifying them and subjecting them to statistical analysis.

When evaluating the effectiveness of services and interventions the value of consultation with service user organisations and organisations representing informal carers must be recognised.

The group also wishes to highlight topics which would benefit from research into their effects on mental health and the potential for primary prevention of any adverse outcomes. These include;

❑ children/adults who are sexually abused

❑ carers of people suffering from chronic mental or physical health problems

❑ individuals who receive genetic counselling.

Once robust research evidence is available the findings should be brought into clinical practice without delay.

7.2 Guidance for purchasers

It is recommended that:-

1. Purchasers ensure that their mental health strategies address primary prevention of mental health problems.

2. Purchasers should develop alliances with other agencies such as national government, local authorities, educational establishments, employers, voluntary organisations and organisations representing service users and carers to:

    a. Highlight the potentially adverse effects on mental health of social and economic factors eg. unemployment, poor housing or homelessness, stress in the work place.

    b. Influence the development of policies, services and actions which have beneficial effects on mental health.

3. Purchasers should build high quality evaluative research into any new primary preventive mental health intervention for which insufficient evidence of effectiveness is currently available, and may need to collaborate with others to do so.

4. Where purchasers currently purchase a service of unproven effectiveness they should not extend the service until further work has been undertaken to clarify the effectiveness of the service.

5. Purchasers should not begin or continue to purchase primary preventive mental health interventions that have been shown to be ineffective.

7.3   Dissemination

The group suggests that the conclusions and recommendations of this report are made widely available and that the following individuals/organisations receive a copy of the full report:-

Heads of Scottish Office Departments other than Home and Health

The Department of Health

General Managers of Health Boards

Trust Chief Executives

Directors of Public Health

The Royal College of General Practitioners

The Royal College of Psychiatrists

The Royal College of Nursing

Directors of Social Work

Voluntary Organisations - Various

Chairpersons of Area Medical Committees, GP Sub-Committees and Area Nursing and Midwifery Committees

Clinical Directors of NHS Trusts

University Departments of Mental Health, General Practice, Social Work and Nursing Studies

Chief Administrative Nursing Officers

Directors of Nursing Services

District Nursing Association

Scottish Health Visitor Association

Professional Head of Scottish Community Psychiatric Nurses

National Association of Fundholding Practices

Primary Care Administrators for distribution to each general practice

Mental Welfare Commission for Scotland

Scottish Health Advisory Service

Scottish Branch of the British Psychological Society Clinical Division

Chairpersons of Child Protection Committees

8. REFERENCES

1. Goldberg D, Huxley P. Mental illness in the community. London: Tavistock, 1980.

2. The Health of the Nation. Key Area Handbook: Mental Illness. London: Department of Health, 1993.

3. OPCS Surveys of psychiatric morbidity in Great Britain. Report 1. The prevalence of psychiatric morbidity among adults living in private households. London: HMSO, 1995.

4. Newton J. Preventing mental illness in practice. London: Routledge and Kegan Paul, 1992.

5. Rose G. Sick individuals and sick populations. Int J Epidemiology 1985; 14(1): 32-38.

6. Rutter M, Smith D. Psychosocial disorders in young people. Chichester: Wiley, 1995.

7. Rose G. The Strategy of Preventive Medicine. Oxford: Oxford University Press, 1992.

8. Gunnell D. The Potential for Preventing Suicide. University of Bristol: Health Care Evaluation Unit, May 1994.

9. Royal College of Psychiatrists. Prevention in Psychiatry. Council Report 21. London: March 1993.

10. Kendell R E, Zealley A K. Companion to psychiatric studies. Fifth Edition. Edinburgh: Churchill-Livingstone, 1993.

11. Goldberg D, Williams P. A user's guide to the General Health Questionnaire. Windsor: NFER-NELSON, 1988.

12. Smith R. Unemployment: here we go again. BMJ 1991; 302: 606-607.

13. Third Glasgow Monica Risk Factors Survey (personal communication, Dr Caroline Morrison)

14. Mausner J S, Kramer S. Epidemiology - An Introductory Text. Philadelphia: WB Saunders Company, 1985.

15. Hosman C, Veltman N. Prevention in Mental Health. Utrecht: Landelijk Centrum GVO, 1994.

16. Newton J. Preventing mental illness. London: Routledge and Kegan Paul, 1988.

17. McGuire J, Earls F. Prevention of psychiatric disorders in early childhood. J Child Psychol Psychiat 1991; 32(1): 129-154.

18. Roberts M C, Peterson L. Prevention of Problems in Childhood. Psychological Research and Applications. New York: John Wiley and Sons, 1984.

19. Yoshikawa H. Prevention as cumulative protection: effects of early family support and education on chronic delinquency and its risks. Psychological Bulletin 1994; 115(1): 28-54.

20. Huxley P, Warner R. Primary prevention of parenting dysfunction in high-risk cases. Amer J Orthopsychiat 1993; 63(4): 582-588.

21. Farrington D P. Delinquency prevention in the 1980s. J Adolescence 1985; 8: 3-16.

22. Cox A D, Pound A, Mills M et al. Evaluation of a home visiting and befriending scheme for young mothers: Newpin J Roy Soc Med 1991; 84: 217-220.

23. Pound A, Mills M. A pilot evaluation of NEWPIN, a home-visiting and befriending scheme in South London. Newsletter of the Association of Child Psychol and Psychiat 1985; October: 13-15.

24. Johnson D L, Breckenridge J N. The Houston Parent-Child Development Centre and the primary prevention of behaviour problems in children. Am J Community Psychol 1982; 10(3): 305-316.

25. Ramey C T, Campbell F A. Preventive education for high-risk children: cognitive consequences of the Carolina Abecedarian Project. Am J Mental Deficiency 1984; 88(5): 515-523.

26. Darmstadt G L. Community-based child abuse prevention. Social Work 1990; 35(6): 487-489.

27. Child Protection: the impact of the Child Development Programme. University of Bristol, Early Childhood Development Unit: 1992.

28. Barth R P. An experimental evaluation of in-home child abuse prevention services. Child Abuse and Neglect 1991; 15: 363-375.

29. Olds D L, Henderson C R, Chamberlin R et al. Preventing child abuse and neglect: a randomised trial of nurse home visitation. Paediatrics 1986; 78(1): 65-78.

30. Shure M B, Spivack G. Interpersonal problem solving in young children: a cognitive approach to prevention. Am J Comm Psychol 1982; 10(3): 341-356.

31. Elias M J, Gara M A, Schuyler T F et al. The promotion of social competence: longitudinal study of a preventive school-based program. Amer J Orthopsychiat 1991; 61(3): 409-417.

32. Hawkins J D, Von Cleve E, Catalano R F. Reducing early childhood aggression: results of a primary prevention program. J Am Acad Child Adolesc Psychiatry 1991; 30(2): 208-217.

33. Bry B H. Reducing the incidence of adolescent problems through preventive intervention: One and five year follow up. Am J Community Psychol 1982; 10(3): 265-2-.

34. Felner R D, Ginter M, Primavera J. Primary prevention during school transitions: social support and environmental structure. Am J Comm Psychol 1982; 10(3): 277-290.

35. Quinton D, Rutter M, Liddle C. Institutional rearing, parenting difficulties and marital support. Psychol Med 1984; 14: 107-124.

36. Garland A F, Zigler E. Adolescent suicide prevention. Current research and social policy implications. American Psychologist 1993; 48(2): 169-182.

37. Low B P, Andrews S F. Adolescent suicide. Adolescent Medicine 1990; 74(5): 1251-1264.

38. Overholser J, Evans S, Spirito A. Sex differences and their relevance to primary prevention of adolescent suicide. Death Studies 1990; 14: 391-402.

39. Ciffone J. Suicide prevention: a classroom presentation to adolescents. Social Work 1993; 38(2): 197-203.

40. Orbach I, Bar-Joseph H. The impact of a suicide prevention program for adolescents on suicidal tendencies, hopelessness, ego identity, and coping. Suicide and life-threatening behaviour 1993; 23(2): 120-129.

41. Shaffer D, Garland A, Vieland V et al. The impact of curriculum-based suicide prevention programs for teenagers. J Am Acad Child Adolesc Psychiatry 1991; 30(4): 588-596.

42. Klingman A, Hochdorf Z. Coping with distress and self harm: the impact of a primary prevention program among adolescents. Journal of Adolescence 1993; 16: 121-140.

43. Vieland V, Whittle B, Garland A et al. The impact of curriculum-based suicide prevention programs for teenagers: an 18 month follow-up. J Am Acad Child Adolesc Psychiatry 1991; 30(5): 811-815.

44. Elliot S A, Sanjack M, Leverton T J. Parent groups in pregnancy, in Gottlieb B H (Ed). Marshalling social support. London: Sage, 1988.

45. Murray L. The impact of postnatal depression on infant development. J Child Psychol Psychiat 1992; 33(3): 543-561.

46.   Cummings E M, Davies P T. Maternal depression and child development. J Child Psychol Psychiat 1994; 35(1): 73-112.

47.   Cox J L, Holden J M, Sagovsky R. Detection of postnatal depression. Br J Psychiat 1987; 150: 782-786.

48.   Gerrard J, Holden J M, Elliot S A et al. A trainer's perspective of an innovative programme teaching health visitors about the detection, treatment and prevention of postnatal depression. J Adv Nurs 1993; 18: 1825-1832.

49.   Scott D. Early identification of maternal depression as a strategy in the prevention of child abuse. Child Abuse and Neglect 1992; 16: 345-358.

50.   Holden J M, Sagovsky R, Cox J L. Counselling in a general practice setting: controlled study of health visitor intervention in treatment of postnatal depression. BMJ 1989; 298: 223-226.

51.   Jacobs S, Kim K. Psychiatric complications of bereavement. Psychiatric Annals 1990;20(6):314-317.

52.   Parkes C M. Bereavement counselling: does it work? BMJ 1980; 281: 3-6.

53.   Parkes C M. Evaluation of a bereavement service. J Prev Psychiat 1981; 1(2): 179-188.

54.   Raphael B. Preventive intervention with the recently bereaved. Arch Gen Psychiat 1977; 34: 1450-1454.

55.   Silverman P R. The widow-to-widow program. Mental Hygiene 1969; 53(3): 333-337.

56.   Siegel K, Mesagno F P, Christ G. A prevention program for bereaved children. Amer J Orthopsychiat 1990; 60(2): 168-175.

57.   Parkes C M. Risk factors in bereavement: implications for the prevention and treatment of pathologic grief. Psychiatric Annals 1990;20(6):308-313.

58.   Duke S. Establishing a bereavement service. Nursing Standard 1990; 5(10): 34-37.

59.   Maguire P, Tait A, Brooke M et al. Effect of counselling on the psychiatric morbidity associated with mastectomy. BMJ 1981; 281: 1454-1456.

60.   Greer S, Moorey S, Baruch J D R et al. Adjuvant psychological therapy for patients with cancer: a prospective randomised trial. BMJ 1992; 304: 675-680.

61.   McFarlane A C. The aetiology of post-traumatic morbidity: predisposing, precipitating and perpetuating factors. Br J Psychiatry 1989; 154: 221-228.

62.   Alexander D A, Wells A. Reactions of police officers to body-handling after a major disaster. A before and after comparison. Br J Psychiatry 1991; 159: 547-555.

63.   Alexander D A. Stress among body handlers. A long term follow up. Br J Psychiatry 1993; 163: 806-808.

64.   Samter J, Fitzgerald M L, Braudaway C A et al. Debriefing: from military origin to therapeutic application. J Psychosocial Nurs 1993; 31(2): 23-27.

65.   Deahl M P, Gillham A B, Thomas J et al. Psychological sequelae following the Gulf War. Factors associated with subsequent morbidity and the effectiveness of psychological debriefing. Br J Psychiat 1994; 165: 60-65.

66.   Hoiberg A, McCaughey B G. The traumatic after-effects of collision at sea. Am J Psychiat 1984; 141(1): 70-73.

67.   Raphael B, Meldrum L, McFarlance A C. Does debriefing after psychological trauma work? BMJ 1995; 310: 1479-1480.

68. Bloom B L, Hodges W F, Caldwell R A. A preventive programme for the newly separated: initial evaluation. Am J Community Psychol 1982; 10(3): 251-264.

69. Bloom B L, Hodges W F, Kern M B, McFaddin S C. A preventive programme for the newly separated: final evaluations. Amer J Orthopsychiat 1985; 55(1): 9-26.

70. Stolberg A L, Garrison K M. Evaluating a primary prevention programme for children of divorce. Am J Community Psychol 1985; 13(2): 111-124.

71. Pedro-Carroll J L, Cowen E L. The children of divorce intervention programme: an investigation of the efficacy of a school-based prevention programme. J Consulting and Clinical Psychol 1985; 53(5): 603-611.

72. Warr P, Jackson, P, Banks M. Unemployment and mental health: some British studies. J Social Issues 1988; 44(4): 47-68.

73. Hammer T. Unemployment and mental health among young people: a longitudinal study. J Adolescence 1993; 16: 407-420.

74. Finlay-Jones R A, Eckhardt B. Psychiatric disorder among the young unemployed. Aust. and NZ J Psychiatry 1981; 15: 265-270.

75. Platt S D. Unemployment and suicidal behaviour: a review of the literature. Social Science and Medicine 1984; 19: 93-115.

76. Platt S D, Kreitman N. Trends in parasuicide and unemployment among men in Edinburgh. BMJ 1984; 289: 1029-1032.

77. Platt S D, Dyer J A T. Psychological correlates of unemployment among male parasuicides in Edinburgh. Br J Psych 1987; 151: 27-32.

78. Pritchard C. Is there a link between suicide in young men and unemployment? Br J Psych 1992; 160: 750-756.

79. Hawton K, Fagg J, Simkin S. Female unemployment and attempted suicide. Br J Psych 1988; 152: 632-637.

80. Turner J B, Kessler R C, House J S. Factors facilitating adjustment to unemployment: implications for intervention. Am J Comm Psychol 1991; 19(4): 521-542.

81. Caplan R D, Vinokur A D, Prince R H et al. Job seeking, re-employment and mental health: a randomised field experiment in coping with job loss. J Applied Psychol 1989; 74: 759-769.

82. Vinokur A D, Price R H, Caplan R D. From field experiments to programme implementation: assessing the potential outcomes of an experimental intervention programme for unemployed persons. Am J Comm Psychol 1991; 19: 543-562.

83. Faculty of Public Health Medicine. Royal Colleges of Physicians. Alcohol and the Public Health. London: MacMillan, 1991.

Appendix A

Terminology

There are difficulties with terminology in the area of mental health, particularly in the use of terms such as 'illness' and 'disease'. Two definitions are recognised internationally; the International Statistical Classification of Diseases and Related Health Problems (ICD-10) developed by the World Health Organisation (WHO) and the Diagnostic and Statistical Manual of Mental Disorders (DSM-IV) developed by the American Psychiatric Association.

ICD-10 uses the term disorder. It states 'disorder is not an exact term, but it is used here to imply the existence of a clinically recognisable set of symptoms or behaviour associated in most cases with distress and with interference with personal functions. Social deviance or conflict alone, without personal dysfunction, should not be included in mental disorder as defined here.'

DSM-IV also uses the term disorder. It states 'each of the mental disorders is conceptualized as a clinically significant behavioural or psychological syndrome or pattern that occurs in an individual and that is associated with present distress (e.g. a painful symptom) or disability (i.e. impairment in one or more important areas of functioning) or with a significantly increased risk of suffering death, pain, disability, or an important loss of freedom. In addition, this syndrome or pattern must not be merely an expectable and culturally sanctioned response to a particular event, for example, the death of a loved one. Whatever its original cause, it must currently be considered a manifestation of a behavioural, psychological, or biological dysfunction in the individual. Neither deviant behaviour (e.g. political, religious, or sexual) nor conflicts that are primarily between the individual and society are mental disorders unless the deviance or conflict is a symptom of a dysfunction in the individual, as described above.'

Members of the group discussed at length the terminology to be used in this document. Whilst acknowledging the above definitions, it was felt that the document does not exclusively refer to those disorders defined as above. For example, in the section on the under fives and their families certain interventions lead to beneficial effects on cognitive development, school achievement and delinquent behaviour. Furthermore, it was accepted that certain terms such as 'illness' are not acceptable to many groups. Therefore we agreed to use the term 'mental health problems' which will be used throughout the document except where there are direct quotes from other authors.

Appendix B

Membership of the Primary Prevention Group

Dr Karen Foster (Chair)	Consultant in Public Health Medicine Grampian Health Board
Professor David Alexander	Professor of Mental Health University of Aberdeen
Mr James Cleary	Community Psychiatric Nurse The Royal Edinburgh Hospital, Edinburgh
Dr Mary Higgins	General Practitioner, Stirling
Mr George Kappler	Social Work Officer, Mental Welfare Commission for Scotland, Edinburgh
Mr Ian Malcolm	Business Manager, Mental Health Directorate Central Scotland Healthcare NHS Trust, Larbert
Mr John McDonald	Castle Group, Edinburgh
Dr Jenny Secker	Development and Evaluation Officer Health Education Board for Scotland

Secretariat

Ms Aileen Campbell	CRAG Secretariat, SOHHD (until 28 April 1995)
Ms Annmarie MacRury	CRAG Secretariat, SOHHD

Acknowledgement

The group would like to acknowledge the contribution of Sir Michael Rutter, of the Department of Child and Adolescent Psychiatry at the Institute of Psychiatry in reviewing a draft version of this document.

Appendix C

Consultation

The following commented on the document in writing:

Dr Kenneth Aitken	Principal Clinical Neuropsychologist, Edinburgh Sick Childrens Hospital
Dr Patricia Donald	Honorary Secretary, Scottish Council, Royal College of General Practitioners
Dr E Gadd	Senior Medical Officer, Department of Health, London
Dr A Jacques	Medical Commissioner, Mental Welfare Commission for Scotland
Mr Robin Laing	Director, Scottish Association of Mental Health
Mr Tom Leckie	Social Work Services Inspector St Andrew's House
Mr Colin Mackenzie	Convener Association of Directors of Social Work
Dr Stephen Platt	Director of Development and Evaluation, Health Education Board for Scotland until November 1995, now Department of Behavioural Science, University of Edinburgh

The Royal College of Psychiatrists (Scotland)

Dr Roger Simmons	Senior Medical Officer, Scottish Office
Dr Andrew Walker	Health Economist, Greater Glasgow Health Board
Prof Graham Watt	Head of Department, Department of General Practice, University of Glasgow